QUOKKA

By Jenna Grodzicki

BEARPORT
PUBLISHING

Minneapolis, Minnesota

Credits

Cover and title page, © Sunny Ikigai/Shutterstock; 3, © Ines Porada/Adobe Stock; 4–5, © Kaleidosnaps/Wirestock Creators/Adobe Stock; 7, © Sahara Frost/Shutterstock; 9, © Susan Flashman/Adobe Stock, Hello UG/Adobe Stock; 10–11, © Simon/Adobe Stock; 13, © Josedlac/Shutterstock; 14, © Arun Sankaragal/Shutterstock; 15, © Susan Flashman/Shutterstock; 16, © Osprey Creative/Shutterstock; 17, © Hideaki Edo/iStock; 19, © Avico Ltd/Alamy; 21, © Damian Lugowski/Shutterstock; 22, © Arvila/Shutterstock, ozflash/iStock; 23, © dudlajzov/Adobe Stock.

Bearport Publishing Company Product Development Team
President: Jen Jenson; Director of Product Development: Spencer Brinker; Managing Editor: Allison Juda; Associate Editor: Naomi Reich; Senior Designer: Colin O'Dea; Associate Designer: Elena Klinkner; Associate Designer: Kayla Eggert; Product Development Specialist: Anita Stasson

Library of Congress Cataloging-in-Publication Data

Names: Grodzicki, Jenna, 1979- author.
Title: Quokka / by Jenna Grodzicki.
Description: Minneapolis, Minnesota : Bearport Publishing Company, [2024] |
  Series: Library of awesome animals | Includes bibliographical references
  and index.
Identifiers: LCCN 2023001605 (print) | LCCN 2023001606 (ebook) | ISBN
  9798885099981 (library binding) | ISBN 9798888221815 (paperback) | ISBN
  9798888223130 (ebook)
Subjects: LCSH: Quokka--Juvenile literature. | Quokka--Life
  cycles--Juvenile literature.
Classification: LCC QL737.M35 G76 2024 (print) | LCC QL737.M35 (ebook) |
  DDC 599.2/2--dc23/eng/20230208
LC record available at https://lccn.loc.gov/2023001605
LC ebook record available at https://lccn.loc.gov/2023001606

For more information, write to Bearport Publishing, 5357 Penn Avenue South, Minneapolis, MN 55419.

Contents

AWESOME
Quokkas!

A quokka (KWOH-kuh) makes its way down a path, looking for a shady spot to rest. **HOP, HOP!** With their small bodies and famous smiles, quokkas are awesome!

QUOKKAS ARE A TYPE OF WALLABY. THEY ARE CLOSELY RELATED TO KANGAROOS.

Happy Hopper

Quokkas are furry little creatures with small, round ears and long, thin tails. But they are perhaps best known for their cute smiles. Of course, quokkas aren't actually smiling. They only look like they are because of the way their faces are shaped. Their mouths stretch far back, giving them the appearance of a wide grin.

QUOKKAS ARE OFTEN CALLED THE HAPPIEST ANIMALS IN THE WORLD BECAUSE OF THE WAY THEY LOOK.

All in the Family

These great grinners live mostly in small family groups led by the largest **male**. At night, the **nocturnal** creatures go out in groups to look for food.

During the day, however, a quokka family spreads out. Each member heads to a different shady spot to snooze. *ZZZ!* Usually, each quokka will use the same spot every day.

QUOKKA FAMILIES ARE USUALLY PEACEFUL, BUT SOMETIMES MALES FIGHT FOR THE BEST SHADE.

Home Sweet Home

Shade is a must for quokkas trying to beat the heat. These animals live in Australia. Most can be found on two islands where it is often quite warm. Quokkas can make their homes in swamps, forests, or near riverbanks—anywhere with plenty of plants and trees for that all-important shade.

QUOKKAS CREATE PATHS THROUGH THE THICK **VEGETATION** TO MAKE IT EASIER TO HOP FROM PLACE TO PLACE.

What's for Dinner?

All that plant life is also great when quokkas are hungry. They chow down on meals of leaves, grasses, stems, and bark. **YUM!** Quokkas will also eat seeds and berries when they can. But if food and water are hard to find, quokkas can go for a long time without them. The critters can live off fat stored in their tails!

QUOKKAS SOMETIMES CLIMB TREES TO GET TO A TASTY SNACK.

Danger!

To avoid becoming another animal's dinner, quokkas need to be on the lookout for **predators**. They quickly hop away if they spot red foxes, wild dogs called dingoes, or birds of prey.

However, the biggest danger to quokkas is the loss of their **habitat**. Humans have cleared away land where these animals live. Because of this, quokkas are in danger of becoming **extinct**.

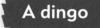
A dingo

QUOKKAS CAN HOP AWAY FROM DANGER AT SPEEDS OF NEARLY 20 MILES PER HOUR (32 KPH).

Furry Rescue

There are fewer than 15,000 quokkas left in the wild. Most are found on Rottnest Island. Many people travel there to visit these cuties. The island has groups that teach visitors about quokkas and ways to help them. This extra attention may help protect the quokkas' homes.

ROTTNEST ISLAND GIVES VISITORS TIPS ON HOW TO TAKE SELFIES WITH QUOKKAS WHILE KEEPING THE ANIMALS SAFE.

Meet the Joey

Once or twice a year, male and **female** quokkas **mate**. A baby quokka, called a **joey**, is born about one month later. The tiny baby is blind and hairless. It crawls into its mother's pouch where it will drink milk from her body and grow for the next six months.

QUOKKAS ARE **MARSUPIALS**. AS BABIES, THEY LIVE IN A POUCH ON THEIR MOTHER'S BODY.

Growing Up

After the joey grows big enough, it will leave its mother's pouch. But until the joey is about a year old, the young quokka and its mother stay together. The mother teaches the joey how to find its own food. When it is about a year and a half old, the quokka is ready to live on its own.

QUOKKAS LIVE FOR ABOUT 10 YEARS IN THE WILD.

QUOKKAS ARE AWESOME!
LET'S LEARN EVEN MORE ABOUT THEM.

Kind of animal: Quokkas are mammals. Most mammals have fur, give birth to live young, and drink milk from their mothers as babies.

Size: Quokkas are about 16 to 21 inches (40 to 54 cm) long. That's about the same size as a house cat.

More marsupials: There are more than 250 types of marsupials, including kangaroos, koalas, and wombats.

QUOKKAS AROUND THE WORLD

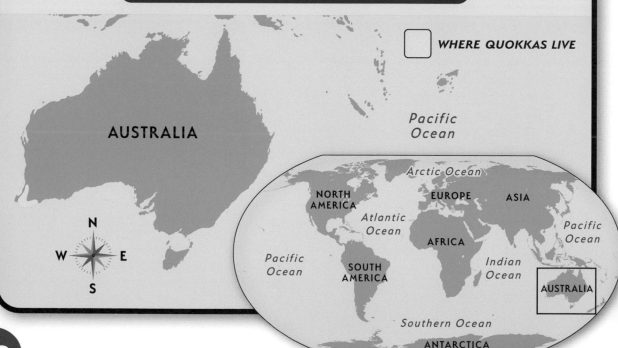

☐ **WHERE QUOKKAS LIVE**

AUSTRALIA

Pacific Ocean

N
W E
S

Arctic Ocean

NORTH AMERICA

EUROPE

ASIA

Atlantic Ocean

Pacific Ocean

AFRICA

Pacific Ocean

Indian Ocean

SOUTH AMERICA

AUSTRALIA

Southern Ocean

ANTARCTICA

Glossary

extinct when a type of animal or plant dies out completely

female a quokka that can give birth to young

habitat a place in nature where an animal normally lives

joey a baby quokka

male a quokka that cannot give birth to young

marsupials animals that carry babies in pouches on their stomachs

mate to come together to have young

nocturnal active mainly at night

predators animals that hunt and eat other animals for food

vegetation different types of plants, including grasses, bushes, and trees

wallaby small members of the kangaroo family

23

Index

Read More

Dickmann, Nancy. *The Smiliest Animals Ever (Awesome Animals).* Mission Viejo, CA: QEB Publishing, 2022.

Jaycox, Jaclyn. *Quokkas (Animals).* North Mankato, MN: Pebble, 2021.

Learn More Online

1. Go to **www.factsurfer.com** or scan the QR code below.
2. Enter "**Quokka**" into the search box.
3. Click on the cover of this book to see a list of websites.

About the Author

Jenna Grodzicki lives on beautiful Cape Cod with her husband and two children. She is both a library media specialist and a writer. She loves to read and go to the beach.